# MY UNIQUE INVESTMENT PLAN

## HIGH LIFETIME INCOME FOR ME
## FABULOUS DEAL FOR MY RENTERS

### John Adams

When Hal Smith, my friend and fellow investor, heard I was writing a book, he asked to write a forward.

**Forward**

John and I play golf together. As we grew to know each other, he began to talk about his idea of investing in property in a bad economy. His idea of rent-to-barter was unique in that it involved no down payment to qualified people. With the housing market in a slump he could borrow money, purchase property, and rent it out at very little over-the-normal rate for renters and still make a substantial profit.

John has a very analytical mind. He showed me page after page of figures showing all the aspects and analysis of how his system worked. John has been investing in real estate as a means to supplement his income for a great many years and has a vast knowledge of property values and resale.

At the time he shared his plan with me, I had some property with limited success at keeping good renters. On John's advice, I advertised my property as rent-to-own with no down payment on Craig's List. I found a wonderful tenant. I explained my motivation to rent it with nothing down; that he must pay for all repairs and maintain the property for 15 years and the property would be his. The rent rate was about $200 more than the going rate, showing a 13% interest rate on the money I had invested in the property.

I purchased a second property in a senior community where you could not rent it out for one year after purchase. John advised me to simply resell it. Again, finding a well-qualified buyer, I sold it with very little down and carried the paper again with a payment much better than rental rate. Plus, there was no upkeep, taxes or HOA dues.

Thank you, John, for giving me such good advice that has proven itself.

Hal Smith

**CHAPTERS**

1. SUMMARY

2. WHY I FELT THE NEED TO INVEST

3. DEVELOPMENT OF A PLAN

4. AN EQUITY LINE OF CREDIT: MY SOURCE FOR MONEY

5. MY PAST EXPERIENCE WITH RENTERS

6. MY PLAN COMPARED TO A LEASE/OPTION PLAN

7. A SCAM ARTIST RENTER AND THE OUTCOME

8. INSURANCE IS OFTEN MISLEADING

9. WHY THIS PLAN BECOMES SAFER WITH TIME

10. WHY THE RECESSION MADE THIS PLAN WORK BETTER

11. WHY THIS PLAN WORKS BETTER FOR THE ELDERLY

12. ADVICE FOR BEING SUCCESSFUL IN ANY ENDEAVOR

13. THIS INVESTMENT COMPARED TO A REVERSE MORTGAGE

14. WHY WORKING FOR YOURSELF WORKS BEST

15. FORMS AND PROCEDURES

16. MY ANALYSIS OF THE RESULTS OF THIS PLAN

## 1. SUMMARY

Most people, when they save for retirement, put the money into a CD, insurance annuity, the stock market, or something of a similar nature. There are two problems with this approach. The first is that any time a large company touches your money they help themselves to a large chunk of it. The second is that the money is not usually available for immediate use. For young families, that may be the only alternative they have. For those in retirement or near it, there is a better approach.

Many people do not think of money working for them, but use what they have saved and hope it will last. In this case, their resources are only receding as they meet their monthly needs.

My approach to investing is to find a way that does not amass money, but instead provides a lifetime monthly income that does not decline when used and does not involve a large company.

I have written this book to show others how this can be done. My approach is to buy houses and rent them to deserving families that cannot buy a home for 12 years (my expected lifetime). I use the money they pay in rent to reduce my loans (which takes about six years) to the point of owning every house free and clear. It is their rent money — not my money — that pays off the mortgages. My renters are motivated to care for and maintain the property—which I do not want to do—because I will trade (barter) their paying all costs, maintenance, and not missing a payment in 12 years for my giving them the house free and clear.

Over the 12 years, I pay taxes and insurance and keep the house in my name. If rent is not paid, I can evict the renter and start a new 12-year deal with another renter. I can also depreciate the house to lower my tax bill. Renters line up to get this deal and from the start, I have monthly income for life.

Many families had their homes foreclosed during the recent recession of 2009 and were forced to rent. They also lost their credit rating and did not have the down payment required to get a loan to buy a home. That put pressure on the rental market and forced rent prices to rise. I developed a plan to help these people and at the same time make a good investment for my family.

It takes a unique set of circumstances to make my plan work well. These were all present at the beginning of the recession. They are: 1. cheap houses from all the foreclosures, 2. low interest rates on loans, 3. some source of investment money, either savings or loans, 4. high demand for rental houses, and 5. a point in time when house prices are more likely to go up in the future than they are to go down. All five of these requirements were present at the beginning of the recession in 2009.

I am placing this summary of the plan as my first chapter so that persons for whom the plan does not fit need read no further, unless they are interested in the ups and downs I encountered in putting this plan into practice.

The basic concept is to rent a home to someone who would like to own a home but is forced to rent because they do not have the credit rating or down payment to qualify for a home loan. For their work, paying all maintenance costs, and never missing a payment, they get the home free and clear in 12 years.

I do not charge any down payment or security deposit. The renter's payments simply start with the first month's rent. At my age (80 years old), I did not want the headaches normally associated with owning or managing rentals. So, part of the agreement is that the renter takes care of all costs related to escrow, repairs, utilities, upkeep, and improvements, as they would if they owned the home.

There is a payment requirement. One missed payment in 12 years requires negotiations. Three missed payments voids the contract. The renter has the following choices: to continue renting though they will not be given the home, they can move out, or I may evict them and start over with a new family. This plan is straight rent with a barter agreement. If they leave, I get more than 12 years' rent: the original renter's and the new renter's 12 years.

This plan is especially good for a person my age because several of the homes I now have will be given to the renters when I am 94 years old. And, the most recent homes I acquired, when I would be 96 years old. Since I may not live that long, my assets have been placed in a Living Trust with my son as the executor. His only job would be to check my bank accounts to make sure payments have been made as well as to call and remind the renter if they have not paid. I give a ten day grace period for payments and work with those who have problems beyond their control, which builds a very a good relationship between me and the renter.

In looking for renters, I try to find people with a good rental payment record, a steady long-term job, and give priority to those with a recommendation from friends or current renters. I also look for people who have enough extra money and skills to improve the property over time. I tell the renter to improve the house, as they are able, so that when they get it in 12 years, it will be worth more. It is like putting money in a savings account and you get to enjoy the improvements before the home is yours.

It is very easy to find renters who want to follow my plan. I give them a copy of the contract and what they will pay in rent based on what I pay for the house. I also tell them to find a house they would like, but one that within their budget. The chart I give them lists home prices in $5,000 increments and the rent associated with that home price.

If they find a home, I look it over carefully and tell them all the improvement costs they will encounter. I have turned down several houses chosen by my renters because of the necessary maintenance and improvement costs. The renters are grateful because I am saving them money on items they did not notice due to lack of experience.

We sign a contract detailing what they will do and what I will do. On the following page is a list of what the renter will do and what I will do.

The income from this investment and how renters have cared for and improved their homes exceeds my expectations. This has been a great investment.

| What I Will Do: | What the Renter Will Do: |
|---|---|
| 1. Buy the home.<br>2. Charge no down payment.<br>3. Charge no security deposit.<br>4. Let them find the home they want.<br>5. Give them all increases in home appreciation.<br>6. Keep the home in my name for 12 years.<br>7. Pay the taxes and insurance on the home for 12 years.<br>8. Give them the home in 12 years, if they have met all requirements.<br>9. Regarding payments, I will work with them on problems beyond their control.<br>10. Give them the proceeds of insurance claims for use to repair the home only.<br>11. Give them a ten-day grace period for payments. | 1. Rent the home for 12 years at the agreed price.<br>2. Never miss a payment (one miss requires negotiations, three misses voids the contract).<br>3. Pay all maintenance costs.<br>4. Pay the title transfer and escrow costs at the end of 12 years.<br>5. Pay all utility costs.<br>6. Pay all costs related to the house except taxes and insurance.<br>7. If they quit paying and void the contract, they agree to leave the property and leave all improvements they have made, which become the property of the Adams Trust.<br>8. Take the property in "as is" condition.<br>9. Agree to keep the property in good repair. |

## 2. WHY I FELT THE NEED TO INVEST

I was born March 14, 1929 on a farm near Driftwood, Oklahoma. At 79 years old, I took stock of my financial situation one day and realized that if I passed away first, my wife would be left with an amount of money that would keep her in good shape financially. But, if she passed away first, I would only be in marginal financial shape.

This was due to the teachers' retirement she had, which would stop at her passing. She would lose some or all of my Social Security, but it was less than half of her retirement amount. I had taken out my retirement earlier to invest. As I mentioned before, my birth in 1929 meant that for the first ten years of my life, we were in the Great Depression. The severe problems caused by the Great Depression were far worse than the recession we have just experienced in 2009. My father and mother were both college graduates. After they were married, my father taught school for one year, but he decided that line of work was not for him. He had an opportunity to buy a farm with a reasonable financial arrangement. The farm was 160 acres, two miles south of Driftwood, Oklahoma, which is approximately 100 miles southwest of Wichita, Kansas. He liked the life of farming better than teaching, but the depression times were hard for everyone. One of the hardships I remember was that my dad lost $100 over one year in the sale of crops, so we had no money to spend on things like ice cream cones and toys. My parents were hard-working people and resourceful, traits I learned from them. With no money, we survived on what we had at the start of the depression: about a dozen milk cows, 100-150 laying hens, 10-15 hogs, and the calves from the milk cows. Dad separated the cream from the milk and we sold the cream to a butter making plant in Enid, Oklahoma (60 miles away). This gave us some money for essentials like shoes, grain feed for the farm animals, and other items we could not make. We got food by a barter system. We traded eggs to the store for things like flour and sugar. We raised wheat so we could have coarse ground wheat for our breakfast cereal.

We ate well because we had a very large garden and my mother canned fruits and vegetables. She also canned beef and chicken, which we had because of the farm cows and chickens. Each year, my father butchered a calf and mother canned most of the meat. We did not have an ice box; few had electricity or refrigerators at that time. My mother also made our clothes from the animal feed sacks. She was an excellent seamstress with an AB degree in Home Making.

I learned a lot about resourcefulness from my parents and I had to practice it as a wood shop teacher. This trait more than any other helped me develop a unique investment plan. It has also made me very organized.

One day the pastor of our church, Dr. Larry Thorson, told me he had seen a three bedroom, two bath house for sale for $50,000. It was hard to believe it was so low because prices had been so much higher before the recession hit. Hearing that news got me started on the path toward my investment plan.

## 3. DEVELOPMENT OF A PLAN

During my lifetime, I have had approximately 125 rental properties as investments and I have learned many lessons along the way. Given my stage in my life, I wanted an investment plan that would work for an 80 year old man. I knew that renting several houses was a full-time job. As the landlord, plumbing, electric, water, or gas problems always seemed to arise just when I had something else planned. My plans became secondary and I had to go help the renter.

I knew that, at 80 years old, I had to solve the following problems or I would no longer be able to utilize my experience as a rental property investor or manager.

1. Where do I get the money to buy the homes?
2. How do you get top dollar for the rental properties?
3. How do you get people to not miss payments?
4. How do you avoid destructive, careless renters?
5. How do you avoid the annoyance of rental management without the high costs of management firms?
6. How do you get renters to repair the damage—and often vandalism—in foreclosed homes?
7. How do you get renters to pay maintenance costs, utilities, and even upgrade the home at their expense?

8. How do you get renters to line up to rent from you?

It seemed almost impossible to achieve all of these goals, so I knew it would take something drastic to do the job. I decided to use my age as an advantage.

My father died at 91.5 years of age. My health is so far very good, so I thought I might last to 93 or 94 with good luck. With that in mind, I planned for a 12-year agreement with my renters.

I solved the question of where to get the money to invest by putting an equity line of credit on my home. I had excellent credit, which I used to my advantage. I asked my bank for an equity line. (I will explore the advantages and disadvantages of an equity line in another chapter.)

They said I qualified for an equity line of $150,000 at 3.25% interest. I asked if they would lower the percentage rate for my good credit if I allowed them to take the monthly payment out of my account automatically. They agreed and gave me a 2.79% interest only payment of $348.75 per month for the $150,000.

I was able to get two houses for the money with a payment of $3,000 per month in rent. I knew that with rental rates high and interest low I could make this a good investment.

I solved all the other problems (2-8 on my list) by using my age as an asset. I told renters who were forced to rent anyway that if they would do the items listed (see chapter one), after 12 years, I would give them the property free and clear.

Before I bought the first home, I did 80 pages of ten-year calculations to make sure I could pay off the mortgages and still have a profit. What I found is that I could pay off the mortgages in approximately six years, which meant that the giving of the houses to the renters would likely be after my death. I solved this problem by putting the houses in our Living Trust and named my son the executor. His only job is to make sure the rent payments are made and to sign over the property at the end of the 12 years. The last houses I put 12-year deals on will go to the renters when I am 96 years old, if I make it that far. It takes approximately six years to clear the mortgages on the houses, so I will have six years of high rental income without any mortgage payments. Collecting the payments should be no problem for my son since people are reluctant to quit paying with only 2 to 4 years remaining before the house is given to them.

  I stated that I did 80 pages of calculations before I bought the first house to be safe and work out the problems. I developed a form for this, which is included as a sample form on pages 18-24. The first sample form has $6,000 spendable income per year, the second with $12,000 spendable. This spendable income refers to the money that can be used after the house mortgages, all living expenses, taxes, and insurance costs are paid off each year.

  After I did all the calculations, I had a strong desire to try this investment. I found that rental rates were about 21% of the house purchase price. Since I had very low costs for the $150,000 I had on the equity line of $348.75 per month, I purchased two houses with rents totaling $3,000 per month. I pay the taxes and insurance on the houses and keep them in my name for the 12 years. This gives me a deduction off my taxes and allows me to depreciate the properties.

  Normally, when properties are depreciated, the IRS gets the amount depreciated back when the houses are sold. Because I would be giving the house to the renter or my Living Trust if I passed away, I do not have to pay the deduction back.

  I also found that a $50,000 house was right on the rent market because house prices that are higher than $50,000 do not generate as much revenue for me. In other words, rent on a $100,000 home is not as high as two $50,000 homes.

When I find a renter that I think would be a good prospect for my plan I give them a copy of the contract and chart showing in $5,000 increments of what the rent would be based on what I have to pay for the house. I also advise them to find a house that is within their budget as paying rent that is too high and stretching one's budget only leads to trouble. I developed a list of things I need to ask the renter before I rent to them. You will find a copy in Chapter 15: Forms and Procedures.

I felt this plan would work well for an 80 year old man because I have no rental home responsibilities. I do not even find the home; they do. It has worked well for me.

**Chart A**

Sample Financial Chart (not my actual numbers, but close)

Date: 1/1/14

Percentage on FIX does not go up, ARM goes up or down ($6,000 spendable per year)

I pay equity lines first because as ARMs (adjustable-rate mortgages) their interest loans can rise. (The interest rates on my loans have not risen in four years due to long recession.)

There are six houses are on this rental plan.

The chart is split into two sections on the following pages.

## Chart A

| Income & Source | Loans & Source | Loans Repaid Amount | New Loan Balance | Loan Monthly cost by lender | Living costs per month and year | Monthly spendable & year spendable | Available monthly loan repay | Monthly cost analysis | Yearly loan repay | Year and my age |
|---|---|---|---|---|---|---|---|---|---|---|
| A. $700 B. $875 C. $1,050 D. $900 E. $875 F. $787 G. $790 H. $800 I. $950 J. $1,688 $9,415 $2,585 other income $144,000 total income | A. $125,000 B. $150,000 C. $60,000 D. $20,000 | Loans repaid in 2013 not on this chart | $125,000 $150,000 $60,000 $70,000 | A. $585 B. $348 C. $275 D. $293 $1,501 | 2,700 x12 $32,400 | $500 per mo $6,000 per yr | 0 present loans repaid at this date | $12,000 -$2,700 living exp. -$1,501 loans -$2,000 tax/insurance -$500 spend $5,299 | $5,299 x12 $63,588 | 2014 84 |
| | Fix A. $125,000 Arm B. $150,000 Fix C. $60,000 Arm D. $70,000 | $63,588 -$63,588 | $125,000 $150,000 $60,000 $6,412 | A. $585 B. $348 C. $275 D. $27 $1,235 | $2,700 x12 $32,400 | $500 per mo $6,000 per yr | $5,565 | $12,000 -$2,700 living exp. -$1,235 loans -$2,000 tax/insurance -$500 spend $5,565 | $5,565 x12 $66,780 | 2015 85 |
| | Fix A. $125,000 Arm B. $150,000 Fix C. $60,000 Arm D. $6,412 | $66,780 -$60,968 -$6,412 | $125,000 $89,032 $60,000 0 (pd) | A. $585 B. $206 C. $275 $1,066 | $2,700 x12 $32,400 | $2,000 per mo $6,000 per yr | $3,734 | $12000 -$2,700 living exp. -$1,066 loans -$2,000 tax/insurance -$500 spend $3,734 | $3,734 x12 $44,808 | 2016 86 |
| | Fix A. $125,000 Arm B. $89,032 Fix C. $60,000 | $44,808 -$44,808 | $125,000 $44,224 $60,000 | A. $585 B. $102 C. $275 $962 | $2,700 x12 $32,400 | $500 per mo $6,000 per yr | $5,838 | $12,000 -$2,700 living exp. -$962 loans -$2,000 tax/insurance -$500 spend 5838 | $5,838 x12 $70,056 | 2017 87 |
| | Fix A. $125,000 Fix B. $89,032 Fix C. $60,000 | $70,056 -$44,226 -$25,830 | $125,000 0 (pd) $34,170 | A. $585 C. $157 $742 | $2,700 x12 $32,400 | $500 per mo $6,000 per yr | $6,058 | $12,000 -$2,700 living exp. -$742 loans -$2,000 tax/insurance -$500 spend $6,058 | $6058 x12 $72,696 | 2018 88 |

## Chart A (continued)

| Income & Source | Loans & Source | Loans Repaid Amount | New Loan Balance | Loan Monthly cost by lender | Living costs per month and year | Monthly spendable & year spendable | Available monthly loan repay | Monthly cost analysis | Yearly loan repay | Year and my age |
|---|---|---|---|---|---|---|---|---|---|---|
| | Ranch sold to renter for --- Fix C. $34,170 | $72,696 - $17,5000 $247,696 -$34,170 (pd) $243,526 | All loans paid | A. 0 B. 0 C. 0 D. 0 | $2,700 x12 $32,400 | $5,612 x12 $67,344 +$118,526 $185,870 | 0 | $12,000 $1,688 loan income lost $10,312 -$2,700 living exp. -$2,000 tax $5,612 | $5,612 x12 $67,344 | 2019 89 |
| | Fix A. $125,000 | - $125,000 (pd) $118,526 | | | $2,700 x12 $32,400 | All bills paid for several years of $67,344 spendable minus higher taxes | | | | 2020 90 |

**Chart B**

Sample Financial Chart (not my actual numbers, but close)

Date: 1/1/14

Percentage on FIX does not go up, ARM goes up or down ($12,000 spendable per year)

I pay equity lines first because as ARMs (adjustable-rate mortgages) their interest loans can rise. (The interest rates on my loans have not risen in four years due to long recession.)

There are six houses are on this rental plan; five houses will be paid off this year.

The chart is split into two sections on the following pages.

## Chart B

| Income & Source | Loans & Source | Loans Repaid Amount | New Loan Balance | Loan Monthly cost by lender | Living costs per month and year | Monthly spendable year | Available monthly loan repay | Monthly cost analysis | Yearly loan repay | Year and my age |
|---|---|---|---|---|---|---|---|---|---|---|
| A. $700<br>B. $875<br>C. $1,050<br>D. $900<br>E. $875<br>F. $787<br>G. $790<br>H. $800<br>I. $950<br>J. $1,688<br><br>$9,415<br>$2,585 other income<br>$144,000 total income | A. $125,000<br>B. $150,000<br>C. $60,000<br>D. $70,000 | Loans repaid in 2013 not on this chart dated 1/1/14 | $125,000<br>$150,000<br>$60,000<br>$70,000 | A. $585<br>B. $348<br>C. $275<br>D. $293<br>$1,501 | $2,700 x12<br>$32,400 | $1,000 per mo<br>$12,000 per yr | 0 present loans repaid at this date | $12,000<br>-$2,700 living exp.<br>-$1,501 loans<br>-$2,000 tax/insurance<br>-$1,000 spend<br>$4,799 | $4,799 x12<br>$57,588 | 2014<br>84 |
| | Fix A. $125,000<br>Arm B. $150,000<br>Fix C. $60,000<br>Arm D. $70,000 | $57,588<br><br>-$57,588 | $125,000<br>$150,000<br>$60,000<br>$12,412 | A. $585<br>B. $348<br>C. $275<br>D. $52<br>$1,260 | $2,700 x12<br>$32,400 | $1,000 per mo<br>$12,000 per yr | $5,040 | $12,000<br>-$2,700 living exp.<br>-$1,260 loans<br>-$2,000 tax/insurance<br>-$1,000 spend<br>$5,040 | $5,040 x12<br>$60,480 | 2015<br>85 |
| | Fix A. $125,000<br>Arm B. $150,000<br>Fix C. $60,000<br>Arm D. $12,412 | $60,480<br><br>-$48,068<br>-$12,412 | $125,000<br>$101,932<br>$60,000<br>$0 (pd) | A. $585<br>B. $236<br>C. $275<br>$1,096 | $2,700 x12<br>$32,400 | $1,000 per mo<br>$12,000 per yr | $5,204 | $12,000<br>-$2,700 living exp.<br>-$1,096 loans<br>-$2,000 tax/insurance<br>-$1,000 spend<br>$5,204 | $5,204 x12<br>$62,448 | 2016<br>86 |
| | Fix A. $125,000<br>Arm B. $101,932<br>Fix C. $60,000 | $62,448<br><br>$62,448 | $125,000<br>$39,484<br>$60,000 | A. $585<br>B. $91<br>C. $275<br>$951 | $2,700 x12<br>$32,400 | $1,000 per mo<br>$12,000 per yr | $5,348 | $12,000<br>-$2,700 living exp.<br>-$951 loans<br>-$2,000 tax/insurance<br>-$1,000 spend<br>$5,349 | $5,349 x12<br>$64,188 | 2017<br>87 |

## Chart B (continued)

| Income & Source | Loans & Source | Loans Repaid Amount | New Loan Balance | Loan Monthly cost by lender | Living costs per month and year | Monthly spendable year spendable | Available monthly loan repay | Monthly cost analysis | Yearly loan repay | Year and my age |
|---|---|---|---|---|---|---|---|---|---|---|
| | Fix A. $125,000 Fix B. $39,484 Fix C. $60,000 | $64,188 -$39,484 -$24,704 | A. $125,000 $0 (pd) C. $35,296 | A. $585 C. $113 $698 | $2,700 x12 $32,400 | $1,000 per mo $12,000 per yr | $5,602 | $12,000 -$2,700 living exp. -$698 loans -$2,000 tax/insurance -$1,000 sp $5,602 | $5,602 x12 $67,224 | 2018 88 |
| | Fix A. $125,000 Fix C. $35,296 A- | -$67,224 - $17,5000 -$35,296 $12,5000 $81,928 | Sold to renter for $175,000 (pd) 0 | All loans paid | $2,700 x12 $32,400 | $5,612 x12 $67,344 +$81,928 $149,272 | | $12,000 $1,688 lost A income $10,312 -$2,700 live -$2,000 tax $5,612 spend | $5,612 x12 $67,344 | 2019 89 |
| Note: I did 80+ of thse with money variations before investing | 0 | 0 | 0 | 0 | $2,700 x12 $32,400 | $67,344 spendable for several years minus higher taxes | 0 | $4,583 | | 2020 90 |

## Sample Financial Status Chart

Date: _____

This chart should help you organize the investments, other income, and how many loans are paid off.

It also shows where you stand financially by month and year and when you will clear all loans.

You should note that your income to expenses gets better as loans are paid off. It is always wise to plan for a better tomorrow as there is always potential for unexpected costs.

Insert the following information into this chart:
- all changes, such as, a change in spendable income, purchase of new home, car, etc.
- total houses owned, total First Trust Deeds, total of houses paid in full

| Income & Source | Loans & Source | Loan Principle Payment Amount by Month & Year | New Loan Balance | Loans monthly cost by lender | Living costs by month and year | Property taxes income tax & insurance by month and year | Monthly cost analysis and titles | Spendable by month and year | Year & Your age |
|---|---|---|---|---|---|---|---|---|---|
|  |  |  |  |  |  |  |  |  |  |
|  |  |  |  |  |  |  |  |  |  |

## 4. AN EQUITY LINE OF CREDIT: MY SOURCE FOR MONEY

| Equity Line of Credit | Ordinary 30-year fixed rate loan |
|---|---|
| 1. No set up loan costs or fees | 1. $2,500 setup cost on my last loan. |
| 2. Payment based on amount you are using | 2. Same monthly payment for the length of the loan. |
| 3. ARM Loan, which means the price can go up or down | 3. Monthly payment remains the same even if you pay down on the principle. |
| 4. Eliminates need for raising money at no cost if not needed | 4. Does not help for use as a rainy day emergency fund. |
| 5. Must be tied to prime rate to keep cost of interest lower than home mortgages | 5. Higher rate than loans tied to the prime rate as large companies use equity loans tied to the prime rate. |
| 6. Ten years interest only. You pay down price if and when you can. After ten years, it converts to a fully amortized 20-year loan at the going rate. | 6. Monthly costs are higher due to being fully amortized with part of the monthly payment going to amortize the loan. |

| Equity Line of Credit | Ordinary 30-year fixed rate loan |
|---|---|
| 7. I can write a check for a $20,000 car costing me $46.50 per month because my equity line rate at Citi Bank is 2.79% interest only. But, I must pay off the principal in ten years or it goes on a regular loan of 20 years. The loan is on the house not the car, but it gives you budget control to meet your needs.<br>8. Usually limited to 60% of the home equity value.<br>9. Works well as a rainy day backup fund. | 7. Cannot be used for any other purchased items.<br><br>Note: I try to have some 30-year regular loans for safety in case rates go up. I pay down principles so fast I can outrun all my ARM loans. (adj. rate mortgages)<br><br>8. Usually, the loan is 80% of the house value |

    My investment plan allows me to pay off $50,000 to $60,000 per year on the principle after paying all bills, taxes, mortgages, and living costs and I have extra to spend as I please. I control my budget, but I must be careful to not waste money when I have it. I need to remember to try to pay all mortgages long before the 12 years when the house must be paid off. Equity lines of credit are a great tool. In August 2014, I will have all rental houses paid off except one.

    Equity lines of credit on the house you live in are lower (mine is 2.79%). My rental house equity lines have been 5.65%, but when the bank saw how much I paid over one year they called me and lowered my rate to 4.5%. They also want to have me take out a loan at 2.99% for 2 years or 3.99% on a regular equity line loan. Banks like people who pay back loans first because it lowers their risk.

## 5. MY PAST EXPERIENCES WITH RENTERS

I have managed approximately 125 renters in my lifetime. Every experience is a learning experience. I have certainly made enough mistakes, but I learned a lot through them. Here are some of the things I learned.

1. Do not rent to someone before checking his or her rental history thoroughly. A thorough examination of a potential renter will save you lots of unexpected problems. It is especially important to contact previous landlords.
2. If you cannot take care of the rentals yourself, you will probably not make money and must rely on prices going up for a profit.
3. Most rental managers are more interested in what they can get out of the deal than what you will make.
4. Watch rental properties and check-in with renters on a regular basis. Some renters destroy properties on purpose.
5. Renters' payments are secondary to repairing their car, appliances, or some special entertainment, so they often miss rental payments.
6. California laws make it hard to evict tenants in a short period of time. Plan on at least three to six months.
7. Renters often stay several months without paying rent before they move out or are evicted.

8. If required to leave, many renters are angry when they leave and feel they are entitled to tear the property up for revenge. I have seen houses with over $25,000 damage.

9. Insurance will pay only part of the damage caused by renters. Insurance companies have write-outs and item limitations that keep you from getting the full cost of the damage.

10. It takes time to rent to someone new and may require you to re-paint and repair, which adds to your costs and extends time without that rental income.

These are the reasons why rent is so high. The owner has to be able to make a profit. That is why my plan works well. It is based on the high cost of rent and avoids these problems by providing renter motivation.

I chose to make my plan straight rent so it would last 12 years. On a rent-to-own plan, the equity build-up would allow the renter, after they had approximately 40% paid, to refinance and I would get only 60% of the value of the property. This amount would not be enough to get a monthly payment equal to the rent I had been receiving. Banks offer loans secured by a down payment of 40% and are more likely to make the loan. A normal down payment is 20%. I am aware that if you have a very high credit rating you can get a lower percent down payment, but that would be a rare occurrence in today's market. I would lose the monthly rent, which I could not replace with only 60% of the original value.

## 6. MY PLAN COMPARED TO A RENT-TO-OWN PLAN

| My Plan | Rent-to-Own |
|---|---|
| 1. Straight rent for 12 years. | 1. Part of the rent payment is applied to building equity. |
| 2. No equity build-up for 12 years. | 2. If a renter leaves after a few years, they have enough equity to sell or refinance as they would usually have the 20% down payment needed to buy or refinance. |
| 3. If a renter leaves early, they have no equity and must leave any improvements they have made. | |
| 4. Renter pays no taxes and insurance. | 3. Renter may pay the taxes and insurance. |
| 5. Renter pays no down payment. | 4. Down payment may be required. |
| 6. Renter pays no security deposit. | 5. Security deposit may be required. |
| 7. Renter pays all maintenance and utility costs. | 6. Renter pays for the house as a portion of the rent. Rent per month is higher. |
| 8. Renter is given the house at normal rent rates. | |
| 9. House remains in my name for 12 years. | 7. House is usually in the renter's name. |

If the house selected is located in a no rent housing area, I put the house in the renters name and tell them the advantages and disadvantages they will have.

| Advantages | Disadvantages |
|---|---|
| 1. House in their name. 2. Build up of equity in the house payment. | 1. Must pay the taxes and insurance costs. 2. Responsible for everything related to the house, as they are the owners. |

In a case like this, first, I calculate the monthly payment I would receive if the house were rented. I also check the amortization book for 12 years and match the two. Then, I hold a first Trust Deed on the property. I would need to foreclose before gaining ownership, if the first Trust Deed payment was not made.

## 7. A SCAM ARTIST RENTER AND THE OUTCOME

If you think you can spot a scam artist, still be cautious. The best scam artists know what you are looking for; they are great actors and can convince you they would be your best renters.

I had a scam artist renter who was a big problem. She told the judge I was in Missouri when the escrow for my purchase of the house was about to close. I was in fact on a one-week vacation with friends in the Seattle area. She had her 25-year-old daughter call me to ask if it was ok for them to turn on the water so they could water outside. When I got returned from vacation, they were in the house without my knowledge or permission. She told the judge the real estate agent had let them into the house. I know this was not true because no real estate agent would do this and incur the liability. It is likely that they broke into the house.

This renter had several scams going and had planned for me to be the next target. Her scams were (I got this from other people she scammed):
1. She took photos of million dollar facilities and put the pictures on Craig's List nationwide with a touching story of how she was running a horse rescue operation. She asked for donations to help support this charity operation. In actuality, the horses were hers and she did not rescue them and turn them over to new owners.

2. She posted an ad, looking for a manager for the horse rescue operation, which was answered by a cowboy from Montana. He came and stayed with them for a short time. She forced him to put the property's utilities bill in his name and pay it. She tried to coerce him into signing over all rights to his Social Security benefits to her. He refused and left. She introduced me to him, telling me he was her cousin, which was not true.

3. She went to farmers markets and swap meets and sold clothes that she said she had sewn. Based on all the boxes I saw — a large truck load, it appeared as though she bought the clothes from Mexico, China, or elsewhere for a cheap price and sold them as her own without permits or other costs required of normal retail operations.

4. When I first met this renter, she told me she had several sources of income. Some proved to be true, some not. The sources of income she listed were:

> a. She sewed and sold clothing. It was true that she sold clothes, but not her homemade clothes.
> b. Her husband did lawn maintenance. True.
> c. She claimed SSI for her daughter and her husband. Her husband was unable to read or write and I don't know about her daughter, but she seemed normal. True.
> d. She told me she and her husband had been hit by a drunk driver and very seriously injured. She said the settlement was for $310,000 for them but because the insurance company refused to pay it was increased to $477,000. She expected to get the money soon and wanted to buy the property. I had a lawyer check but he could find no record of the court cases she described. False.
> e. She applied for government grants to buy the house, but they did not go through. True

Another potential renter wanted the house for $100 per month more than the scam artist renter was paying. This potential renter was the contractor in charge of buildings at the school across the road. I thought the scam artist renter would leave because I offered to forgive all the back rent debt she owed when she vacated the property (approximately $30,000). She said no and that she knew how to keep the property tied up in court for months. It was true that she was knowledgeable about all renters' rights. She knew how to play the courts like a magician.

I finally hired a paralegal to help me evict her. We served the papers and she decided to stall. She said her father had died and the funeral was to be the same time as the court date. The court told her that only I could postpone the eviction because I had brought the eviction. She sent me an email you would expect from a professional con artist. It had the obituary with all their names as well as the date, time, and place of the funeral. I looked it over closely because by now I knew her tricks and there was something strange about the document. The obituary was for a man that had no resemblance to the father whom she said was a lawyer and had taught her all the legal tricks she knew.

I turned her down and she shrugged and said she would see me in court. I could tell from her reaction that it was all a lie.

We met in court and although she owed several thousand dollars in back rent, she knew what the court would accept. She found an old e-mail on which I had transposed the numbers on what she owed and it was just off a few dollars. Because of the discrepancy, the judge said she could not give the eviction order until it was straightened out. So, I started over.

Each time I went to court it cost me $150 plus the paralegal fee of $125, but I paid it and we started over. She pays nothing since those on SSI have free court access.

In the meantime, I had a police officer tell her she

could not have horses on the property because I, as the owner, would be fined if they were not removed. I thought he could help convince her, but she ignored it and did nothing toward removing the horses.

Her reaction was to charge me with harassment and write a 50-page document pleading for the judge to keep me 300 feet from the property. She tried to validate her case by citing all the work they had done. She specifically mentioned the cutting down of a tree with a 10" diameter trunk approximately 30 feet tall because its roots were raising the foundation of the house.

In reality, the tree was 45 feet from the house and there was no root damage to the house. She did not realize that the tree was just off my property on the city parking area. She had cut it down along with one on the neighbor's property without getting permission and used it for firewood.

She was asking that I pay $11,000 for taking the tree down as well as the work they did in the house, but she did not have any receipts. She wanted the judge to allow this money to be the down payment so she could get a loan to buy the house for what I paid for it.

The judge told her that since I owned the property I could make the rules and inspect it as needed. The judge said I could not be forbidden to check my property.

One week later, my renter saw me drive by the house. I did not stop, but she ran out toward the road holding her phone and I could read her lips. She said she was calling the police. I checked and found she had called the police, but no report was made since I was not there when the police arrived.

She decided to charge me with harassment again even though she had not paid any rent for several months and all contracts had expired since the judge said I, as the owner, had rights. But, this time my renter said she was the owner and that I was the lien holder. She was trying to prevent me from driving by on a main road to keep me from seeing her illegal activities.

Before the harassment trial date, I went through the process and brought her to court for eviction. I know the judge was fed up with her coming to court with a trumped up story when the bailiff had her swear to tell the truth a second time after our case was called. She said her legal counsel had told her that seven days to report her response was acceptable, rather than the five days that are required even over a weekend. The judge knew she was lying because legal counsel would know there is a five-day requirement even over a weekend. The judge ordered the plaintiff to move out as quickly as possible.

Regarding her harassment charge against me, she used tricks she knew to postpone the hearing, so she could live on the property without paying rent for a longer time. The first postponement she got was to not accept the judge because lawyers were filling in for overworked judges. The second time the hearing date came up, she did the same thing, but the third time, it was sent to the county court house. It came up in the afternoon of the day I got the eviction verdict in my favor, so she did not show up and I won because she never came to court. In all, I went to court six times before she was evicted and she paid no rent for approximately six months.

I knew they would do all the damage they could when they left so I watched the property. When they started tearing up the yard, I called the sheriff since the home was in the county. He came and she conned him. She told him I had canceled their contract, but she is the one that canceled it for lack of payment. She never mentioned the new contract, which stated that all the improvements they made had to be left. She said they were hers and she was taking them to their new home, which was soon to close escrow. The officer asked if they had been renters, which of course they had been, but were not paying. He would not look at what the contract said. The sheriff insisted that if they had been renters, this dispute was a matter for the courts to decide. He watched while they took out 24 trees and left nothing but holes in the front yard.

I called the officer to come back in the afternoon after they had left to see the destruction both inside and outside the house. He said it was not too bad, that he had seen worse. He also stated that the sheriffs' patrol is spread so thin that they only take care of serious crimes and they let the courts settle civil matters.

I called my insurance company and showed them the pictures of what it was like before they tore it up. In the end, they probably did about $15,000 worth of damage to the property. Insurance paid me $10,000 because of write-outs and limits, such as the number of trees covered. They would cover only 5 of the 24 trees.

I called a realtor who was advertizing 4% fee for selling the property. It was a time when houses had gone up sharply because new houses were not being built and the used homes inventory had fallen very low. We put the house on the market at $140,000. Within a week, he had an offer taking the house "as is." Since I got to keep the $10,000 I got from the insurance company, I ended up making $150,000 from that deal. I had also gotten approximately $17,000 from the renter – 4% of the sale price for selling and few other costs. It turned out very well for me because it was one of the houses I had paid off. It was the most profitable house of all I have. I doubled the price I paid for it in three and a half years.

Crime does not always pay. Had the renter's family paid as intended for eight and a half more years, it would have been theirs, free and clear, worth at least $150,000.

That is not the end of the story. About two months later, I got a call from a lady in Perris about 15 miles west, asking me to detail my experience with this family.

They had come to her seeking a vacant model

home she owned on a few acres of land. They explained to her that they wanted to live in the house and keep horses for one week only until the house they were buying closed escrow.

Of course, their house did not close escrow. The renters refused to move out, planning to stall through the courts and pay no rent. The owner was secretary to an attorney and was able to get them out.

At the end of this chapter, I have enclosed my letter to the judge concerning the final eviction trial. The judge ruled without me showing the letter or saying anything. I had hired an attorney and he said a few words for me. Though the judge did not see the letter, I could tell from her actions that the scam artist renter did not fool her.

This renter's plan can be summarized this way: she planned to pay what is required up front to rent. After getting in the house, she stopped paying rent and dodged payments for a month or two by saying her husband or two children had been hurt or sick. Then, she got another four or five months rent-free by taking bogus cases to court and using stall tactics. Since she lives mostly on SSI for her husband and daughter, whom she claims are retarded, it costs her nothing to go to court. The landlord pays $150 to $500 to go to court, which allows her to stall even before she is taken to court. And, if she loses, she pays nothing because they spend all they receive each month and have no money to pay.

She never realized it, but this situation actually did me a favor. They improved the property, allowing me to have pictures of what was there and got me more from the insurance claim than I would have gotten. They also took good care of the property until prices rose. It is because of people like her that rent prices are so high, and those high prices are the basis for the income I receive each month on my investment plan.

After my renters were evicted, the neighbors

thanked me saying she was noisy and a dictator, telling them what they could and could not do on their property. She used the threat of court action if they did not comply. Since she paid nothing and they would pay $150 to $500 to go to court, she could enforce her demands on them.

Letter to the Judge                    March 26, 2013

Your Honor:

    I feel compelled to write this letter to set the record straight. I rented to the __ family in September of 2009. I offered them an excellent opportunity to get a home in 12 years, free and clear of debt by only paying regular rent, escrow costs, maintenance costs, and all utility bills, but to get the home they could not miss a payment, unless it was excused without voiding the contract. If the contract was voided, I would not give them the home. By doing this, they would be free from saving for a down payment and would get the home, which they would not get if they paid regular rent. They accepted the terms but never lived up to them from the start, but instead have tried to get the courts to give them the property without their paying for it by making up false accusations and lying in court. They have not met the terms of any of the contracts.

    Mr. __ is a very hard worker and has kept the outside in excellent shape. He is easy to talk to and is not aggressive. He is illiterate so Mrs. __ does all the family business. She is very hard to deal with. She constantly makes up false scenarios of things to suit what she wants to do, and lies in court about things that never happened. She filed 2 harassment suits against me. She lost in court because I am the owner so she filed a second suit when she saw me drive by on the street and now she says she owns the property and I am a lien holder. She has never paid anything toward the purchase of the house and could not legally own the property. She never gets permission from the owner for even such things as cutting down a large tree just off the property and one on the neighbor's property for which the neighbor was very angry. She told the court the trees were damaging the foundation, which is impossible since they were 45 feet from the house. I think she used them for firewood. She also put 8 horses on the property without asking. The property is too small for any horses to be allowed. I also think she is conducting a retail business out of the home but have no proof except the neighbor saying people come and go from the home all day long. She uses lawsuits and the courts to stall for time to allow her to live on the property rent-free and board the horses, which she refuses to remove from the property. She also bars me as the owner to have any controls or contact with the property where she carries on illegal activities but says in court they are legal. I as the owner have been notified I will be fined if it continues.

I knew they were not legitimate renters when they made almost no payments for the first ten months. They came up with what I thought was a good excuse after being there 1 month, a serious accident to him, so I gave them an excuse for not paying for 2 months. Now I know from their record the accident was probably a fake. I soon found out that they had no intention of honoring the contract but they refused to leave. The first 10 months they should have paid $14,000, but only paid $2,125. Over the past 3 ½ years they have paid approximately 1/3 of rent amount called for on the contract. They have been there 3 ½ years and are behind the contracted amount over $33,000.

I decided to let them buy the property which they told me they wanted to do, but twice they told me they were approved for a loan but each time it proved to be false and all they were doing was stalling for time to rent without paying. I am the sole owner with my wife, in our living trust and we own the property free and clear. We had loans on the property in the past but they are all paid off.

I have attached the CR&R trash bill which she says is not my concern since it is in her name and she is paying but does not, as I pay them on my tax bill. The present bill stands at $731.81 for a total of $1523.33 including what I have already paid.

In court documents she perjured herself by saying I had yelled and screamed and threatened her family and entered her house without even knocking to threaten her family when none of it was true. What set her off was when I received a notice from the county that horses on the property were not allowed since the lot at 16988 SQ FT. is too small for any horses to be allowed. The notice said I would be fined if the horses were not removed. Since then, she has taken me to court 2 times trying to prevent me from enforcing the ban on horses. She has 8 horses on the property and they are all still there. She tells the inspecting code people the lot is a ½ acre (21780 SQ FT) to get a ruling for 2 horses, but that is not true (the lot is 16988 SQ FT.) and 8 horses are not legal there. It is not legal for any horses to be on the property. Horses are also corralled next to the house. The code says they cannot be closer than 50 feet. She abides by no rules.

In the first harassment trial, you ruled that I, as the owner, could have access to the property. She will not abide by the ruling. Since the first trial, she has called the sheriff when she saw me drive by in the car. I checked with the sheriff's office for the report from the deputy. They told me no report was made and I have not met the deputy. I did not stop, but she filed harassment charges anyway.

My reason for driving by was to check on the property and to contact the neighbor who was selling his property – to see what they were asking and if it might be possible to sell the two parcels of land together. I took no pictures of her horses from the neighbors' property. The neighbor did say that the property had a steady stream of people coming and going to the house, which might indicate they are using the property for some commercial endeavor (which the property is not zoned for). If it is illegal, it may be the reason for her paranoia about me being near the property.

At the present time, the family pays no rent at all. Their last payment was $70 in January 2013. She considers the property hers and feel no rent is required. She also totally excludes me from the property. I have had over 150 renters in my lifetime, but have never encountered a take over specialist with her skill and willingness to lie in court to achieve her ends.

Sincerely yours,
John W Adams, owner of the property at _____

## 8.  INSURANCE IS OFTEN MISLEADING

When I was a young man, my experience with insurance companies was very straightforward, but my experience in recent times has not been good.

I keep insurance on all homes on which I have a loan because the lenders require it. When I have paid off a home, I do not insure it if it is a mobile, but I do try to keep insurance on all my stick built homes. Mobiles are cheaper to replace in a total loss.

Insurance is no longer the good investment it was in years past. Several factors make this so and they include:

1. Insurance companies are driven by greed, high salaries for top company executives, and pressure from stockholders demanding high returns.
2. Insurance companies might drop your coverage, if you make a large claim.
3. Insurance companies raise premiums in years following when a claim is made, often to reclaim within 1 or 2 years all they paid out.
4. The write-outs on insurance policies. I had an insurance policy for one of my houses that was supposed to cover water damage. We had a slow leak that we reported as soon as it was found. However, the insurance company would not pay because in the many fine print pages of the policy, they had a write-out stating they

would pay on claims only when the leak was found immediately and the water turned off immediately. That would mean it would be almost impossible for them to ever pay a claim, but I would still be paying the premium, thinking I had water damage insurance.

5. Limitations are often written into policies saying they will pay only so many of a given item. If you have more, it will be up to you to pay for replacements or repairs.

6. If you live in a low risk fire area like a town or city next to a water source and firemen, they may give you a small discount, but you are not given what you deserve for where you are located. Your house may have very little risk to burn and yet you pay for people who choose to live in high risk forested areas. There are also varying degrees of risk in flood areas and although they give you a small break in the premium, it is nowhere near what relates to your risk.

7. Payment delays cause many who have claims, especially if they are large, to still be waiting after two years. The longer the insurance company keeps your claim money the more they profit.

8. If you have a large claim, you should get an attorney to help you. While hiring an attorney adds to your costs, it will usually get you a fairer settlement.

9. Insurance companies will not insure a house for its value, but insure only two to three times its value. There is an item in the policy saying they will only pay the value of the home at loss, less all the depreciation. The house I paid $91,000 for is now insured for $365,000. They said it is their policy to only insure for more than the actual value.

My experience with insurance companies over the years leads me to believe it is one of the lowest paying investments you can make. Small claims are usually paid because they do not affect the insurance company's bottom line so much and are also smaller due to deductibles. Medium and large claims are a poor investment and require a lawyer.

Catastrophic insurance for something that would wipe you out may be needed, but insurance companies have a higher cost even on these and often refuse to write them. Keep in mind: insurance is always better for the insurance company than it is for you.

## 9. WHY THIS PLAN BECOMES SAFER WITH TIME

This plan becomes safer with time for the owner because the renters become more and more financially invested as the years pass. A person who has rented for six years would be reluctant to walk away from their house when they are on track to own the house in six more years. In other words, my investment plan is safer as time goes on because the impetus for the renter to remain committed to the contract grows.

There are some circumstances that might interfere with the renter's commitment, such as:

1. A job change, forcing a move.
2. Loss of a job.
3. Severe illness with large medical costs.
4. Auto accident, resulting in less income and more costs.
5. The loss of the home or damage from severe weather or other natural disasters, such as an earthquake.

As mentioned previously, when renters have problems beyond their control, I work with them to reach a solution. This sets me and my offer (rent-to-barter) apart from the bank and creates good will with my renters.

A recent experience with one of my renters illustrates this well. This renter had an unexpected health issue and needed an operation. As a result, this person fell behind in paying the neighborhood association fee. She was so far behind that the fee had risen to $600 because they turned the issue over to an attorney. As a result, she was accruing both late fees and attorney fees.

I met with her and told her to pay the fees instead of paying me the monthly rent in order to stop to the climbing debt. I told her to pay me back when she could. Making such arrangements with your renters creates good will and is sometimes more valuable than the money. Soon after we had met, her health improved, allowing her to add $100 to each rent check, which she did for six more months.

I have also followed another course of action in special cases, which is, simply extending the house gift date by the amount of the debt. My income is now large enough that these problems are minor.

Another way I handle forced moves, accidents, and sickness that jeopardize the renter's ability to continue is to allow for a sale of their interest to a buyer who would rent for the remaining years of the contact. In the end, this new renter would get the house after having paid the original renter (in installments or a lump sum) for the years they had in the project.

As I said, this investment becomes safer with time because the prize at the end is so great that people will be willing to make any adjustments needed to reach the goal.

## 10. WHY THE RECESSION MADE THIS PLAN WORK BETTER

Most people buy when they see house prices going up at a rapid rate. That is a poor time to buy because much of the possible gain is lost.

In my lifetime, I have seen a handful of recessions. Economic recessions are a given because of human nature. When things are going well, we tend to think it will last forever. And, things do go well until we find ourselves in a drastic oversupply of goods and services. Then, prices fall to get rid of the oversupply and there are some adverse affects.

When people see prices on items falling rapidly, they panic. Like throwing gas on a fire, the decline continues until we have a recession and finally reach a point when there is an undersupply of goods and services. Near the end of the downturn is the best time to buy.

Some recessions are not so severe and do not last long. Some are severe, like the Great Depression and our recent recession, and last several years. The recent recession of 2009 helped my plan for these reasons:

1. I saw it coming and got an equity line of $150,000, which would cost me nothing if I did not use it.
2. When house prices reached bottom or near bottom, I started to buy. I got "more house" for the money.

3. Rent prices went up because of the high number of foreclosures, driving those families into the rental market, increasing demand, and thus, price. If you were foreclosed on, you could not buy another home for 7-10 years because your credit rating was in ruins. Unless you had cash to buy, you were out of luck.

4. Demand for rental houses was great, but not many have the resources—financial or skills—to buy or manage a rental property. And, when a house stands vacant, there is a greater likelihood for vandalism, resulting in damage that would add to the cost of the house and a less than desirable scenario for a buyer.

5. Supply and demand is what makes money, so I made my demand go up by offering a worthwhile result that attracted people with enough money to fix up a house or the skills to do so. These were the renters I was seeking for my investment plan.

6. The nature of the recession allowed me to use the adjustable rate mortgages (ARM) equity lines of credit because I knew I would have two or three years to pay before house prices went up. With the amount I could pay ($50,000 to $60,000), I could outrun the house prices, if they went up. I also hedged my bet by taking some low interest 30 year fixed loans on a few of the houses to give me a fall back base.

7. Interest rates on the loans I got were very low over an extended period of time. I got 2.79% interest on the $150,000 equity line I started with and a 3.5% fixed rate 30-year loan on one of my house deals.

8. In the bottom of a recession, the chances of house prices going up when times get better is far greater than the chances they will go down, which adds to the safety and security of my investment plan.

## 11. WHY THIS PLAN WORKS BETTER FOR THE ELDERLY

There are two main reasons this plan works better for the elderly. The first is it does not require the skill and energy to be able to maintain, repair, and refurbish rentals. This is helpful to an owner with physical limitations, but it is also helpful because repairs and refurbishments are too costly to hire out and still make a profit. I have tried several forms of providing repair and maintenance (hiring out the work, triple leases, cheap high school labor) and none of them make rental investments an easy thing to do, even for a young rental manager. For the elderly, it is impossible.

The second reason my plan works for the elderly is that it provides a high income for life (given that most people do not live past their mid-90's). So, if a person begins implementing this plan in their early 80's, the house rental income stops at a time when it is no longer needed.

When you get older, you no longer have the physical energy or stamina to do the things you did when you were younger. If your mind is clear, you can make money using your brain.

Using my investment plan, I have been able to make more money in four years than I made while working from 25 to 80 years of age. This demonstrates that the use of the mind and resourcefulness are able to produce more than a job using physical labor and little use of the mind.

Young people can follow this plan and make money, but the income will stop unless they reinvest every four to six years. My calculations indicate that under the worst conditions, it produces a good return with very little effort.

This plan also works better if you have the cash savings available and do not have mortgage expenses.

The figures below will make it clearer. This is an example of a scenario where $50,000 was available to invest.

$50,000 investment
$875 monthly rent
$875 x 144 month in 12 years = $126,000
$126,000 minus $50,000 investment = $76,000
$76,000 ÷ 12 years = $6,333.33 per year
$6,333 ÷ by $50,000 = 12.66% (still a good return)

You can take off a tax deduction for the payment of taxes and insurance, which will vary depending on your tax bracket. However, you can also depreciate the property so there is an offset for this cost, again depending on your tax bracket. Knowing the items you can deduct is essential, if you receive high income.

As you can see, even for a young person with extra money to invest, my investment plan provides a reasonable return with very little effort. Unlike the stock market, you have something tangible—the house and property—in case things go bad. This plan also provides a return not possible elsewhere in a recession like the one we have just experienced. The figures above show that you should be able to get your initial investment back in less than half of the 12 years.

## 12. ADVICE FOR BEING SUCCESSFUL

These tips will help no matter what activity or line of work you decide to follow.

1. Develop a plan for what you want to do.

I learned this as a woodworking teacher. No plan means you will have wasted time and material and make unnecessary mistakes.

2. Get an education and experience related to your plan.

Become an expert in your field. All education will help, but if it is related to your plan, it will help more. Experience in your field is essential.

3. Be resourceful and ready to make changes in your plan.

There are no perfect plans.

4. Be aggressive; go after what you want.

If you wait for success to come to you, be prepared for a long wait.

5. Be willing to work hard.

Success is never easy and impossible for the lazy.

6. Be willing to compromise.

Failure to compromise means no progress.

7. Do not procrastinate.

Procrastination leads to extreme inefficiency because what you should have done today must be done tomorrow when you should be working on tomorrow's job.

8. Recognize an opportunity when you see it and act fast.

Some people see an opportunity and while they are hesitating for fear of failure, someone else snatches it up. Know a good opportunity when it comes and seize it. If you pass on good opportunities, you will never succeed. Knowing a good opportunity comes from experience and knowing what you are looking for before you see it not after.

9. Accept advice from others

You do not have all the good ideas. Listen to the advice of others and weigh it.

10. Help others. Do not be greedy.

If you conduct business in a way that is only good for you, your plan will not succeed. Think from your customer's point of view and how they can benefit.

11. Practice patience.

Get to the goal one step at a time. There are very few people who start at the top. If you are determined to only have immediate success, you probably will not make it.

12. Be persistent.

Persistence wins when all else fails.

13. Give others the benefit of the doubt, but also verify their claims.

Check with others who have had dealings with the

person or business.

14. Be positive in your dealings.
>Being negative fosters anger and antagonism.

15. Express gratitude for the good things that come your way.
>People enjoy working with those who are grateful.

16. Smile.
>It is good for both you and others.

## 13. THIS INVESTMENT PLAN COMPARED TO A REVERSE MORTGAGE

**This Investment Plan:**

1. Helps those forced to rent at minimal cost to them
2. Provides a very large savings plan in that the rent money they would pay anyway goes toward receiving their home at the end of the 12 years with no extra costs except home maintenance.
3. Requires no down payment.
4. Requires no security deposit.
5. Allows them to select the home they want in the area they like.
6. Provides excellent training for budgeting wanted improvements and eventual home ownership.
7. Is designed to make the future better than the present when future costs and needs are an unknown.
8. Is better for you, as the owner, in the long run.

**A Reverse Mortgage:**
(It is wise to remember that large companies have neither morals nor empathy. They are driven by the bottom line.)

1. Very high start-up cost in home, resulting in equity loss.

As I was implementing this plan, home start-up cost was around $15,000, compared to $2,500 for a home loan.

2. Higher interest than a regular loan, which is great for the bank.

3. Pays money now from your equity in a home, but depletes it rapidly. In most cases, the bank will own your home when you are done. This costs the bank only 60 to 75% of your home value because that is what they will require on the origination of the loan.

4. Loan repayment is due when you leave the home. If you do not leave there until you die, the bank usually ends up owning your home.

Our neighbor left her home to try living with her daughter, but wanted to return home after a short while. Although most of her furniture was still in the house, the bank would not let her return. She still lives with her daughter in another state and the bank sold her house.

5. You no longer have a home interest deduction on your taxes. The bank pays their mortgage and charges your equity a fee for making the payment.

6. A reverse mortgage is designed to allow the bank to take your home quickly and get appreciation when home prices go up, if they have used all the home equity.

7. A reverse mortgage is designed to make for a better present time financially, but a worse future because it leaves no room for the unknown.

8. It is better for the bank than it is for you.

## 14. WHY WORKING FOR YOURSELF WORKS BEST

Large companies have neither morals nor empathy. They are driven by the bottom line and pressure from stockholders.

While I was still working, I helped form a family partnership and invested in a triple net lease gas station/store and a large dental office. Both of these worked well and since I was still working, the triple net lease made the investment easy for me. A triple net lease means the person or company leasing pays tax, insurance, maintenance, and cares for the property at his or her own expense.

We had an opportunity to make a $60,000 profit in equity with a large company with apartment houses in Houston on a triple net basis. Many investors were investing there because of Houston's ties to oil companies. I was the major owner (75%) in a family partnership.

In this case, it was a bad investment because the company that had the triple net lease took the money to invest and maintain their property rather than ours. A year or so later when a recession hit, we were in a bad position and were unable to maintain the property, eventually losing $500,000 in equity as the property went back to the lender.

A few years later, our family partnership built

seven nice condos in Orange County, California, but a recession started just as we finished. We sold all seven by carrying paper on the down payment from our equity in the property so that the condo buyers could get loans on their condos.

When the recession caused the value of the condos to fall below the loans the condo buyers had gotten, we were wiped out. We sued the condo owners for our loans, but winning a lawsuit and collecting money are two different things when those who owe cannot pay. In that situation, our partnership lost approximately $500,000 again. Needless to say, I learned a lot and have been more cautious in my investing. I have put many safeguards and fall back plans into my investment plan.

I no longer invest with a partnership and I now figure carefully the worst-case scenario. If I can live with the worst case I can imagine, I go ahead with the investment. I have learned that if you invest alone and are not dependent on the actions, needs, and desires of other people, you can move faster and cause fewer problems than with any partnership. I am sure that the education I received by making wrong choices has been a great help to me now.

Obviously, we did not always make badly timed investments or our family partnerships would not have been able to invest as we did. One of the great investments for the family when our kids were growing up was a six bedroom, four bath estate on three and a half acres with a gate house and a guest house. I, being a wood shop teacher, built kitchens for both the guesthouse, which was near the lodge, and the gatehouse, which was some distance away near the road. It was our mountain retreat in Idyllwild, California.

We had the lodge 13 years and used it for family vacations, but we also rented to large church groups and others on weekends to help defray the costs. (Those experiences are another book.) We made it a family tradition to have a reunion at the lodge for Thanksgiving, but when the kids grew up and the upkeep became too much for me, we sold it for four and a half times what we paid for it. It was a nice profit and a great investment.

When only one person is making the decisions about an investment property or situation, it is much easier to manage. My advice is investing alone is better than investing through a partnership.

## 15. FORMS AND PROCEDURES

When a person comes to you seeking one of your homes, the following questions and their answers will help you make a selection. You cannot help everyone.

1. Where are you presently renting? Get the address and how long they have been there.
2. How much are you paying for rent?
3. Have you ever missed a payment? If so, why?
4. Who is your present landlord?
5. What is your landlord's phone number?
6. What homeowner skills do you have?
7. How much savings (excess spendable resources) do you have to maintain a home?
8. What is your job?
9. What is your take home pay?
10. If it is a couple: do both of you work?
11. If the family has children: who cares for the children and what is the cost of childcare?
12. How long have you been at this job?
13. Is it a permanent job or temporary?

You may think of other questions, but answers to these will give you a basic idea of whether or not to rent to this person or family. If this family is selected as your renter, give them the following chart and the reminder to look only at homes that match the amount they can afford in rent. I always take the price of the house and multiply it times 21% to establish the yearly rent. Dividing by 12 months gets the monthly rent.

|  | What I pay for the home: | What you will pay in rent (per month): |
|---|---|---|
| Mobile homes (only in areas where land is included) | $40,000<br>$45,000 | $700<br>$787.50 |
| Stick-built homes | $50,000<br>$55,000<br>$60,000 | $875<br>$962.50<br>$1050 |

# CONTRACT

This contract is for the rent and the bartering services for a gift of the property at the end of 12 years, if all terms of the services rendered have been met. It is for the property located at _____ and is between _____, the renter and _____, the present owner.

| WHAT THE OWNER WILL DO: | WHAT THE RENTER WILL DO: |
|---|---|
| 1. Buy the home.<br>2. Charge no down payment.<br>3. Charge no security deposit.<br>4. Let the renter find the home.<br>5. Give the renter all home appreciation.<br>6. Keep the home in the owner's name for 12 years.<br>7. Pay the tax and insurance for 12 years.<br>8. Give the renter the home in 12 years if all renter obligations have been met.<br>9. Work with the renter on problems beyond their control, if owner is notified.<br>10. Give them the proceeds of insurance claims for damage for the repair of the property only.<br>11. Give a ten-day grace period for a missed payment. | 1. Rent for 12 years at the agreed price of _____ per month based on property value.<br>2. Never miss a payment (one miss will require negotiations, three misses voids the contract). (see negotiations below)<br>3. Pay all costs related to the house such as, final title transaction, utilities, maintenance, etc., except the property tax and insurance.<br>4. If renter leaves or contract is voided, all improvements made to the property are the property of the owner.<br>5. Take the property in (as is) condition.<br>6. Agree to keep the property in good repair.<br>7. Select the day of the month they wish to pay. |

_____    _____
Owner                              Date

_____    _____
Renter                             Date

Negotiations:
If a payment is missed, the renter can:
1. Pay $100 per month more for rent and keep the years he has paid.
2. Pay his present rental rate and start a new 12 years.
3. Move out.
4. Rent at the present rate, but will not get the house.
5. If three payments are missed, the renter must move out.

## 16. MY ANALYSIS OF THE RESULTS OF THIS PLAN

This plan has been the best investment I have ever made for these reasons:

1. The timing was perfect.
2. The recession was long, keeping interest rates low.
3. I was able to get money to invest cheaply.
4. Many houses went into foreclosure, forcing more people toward the rental market.
5. Rentals were in demand, keeping rental rates high.
6. The plan relieved me of the problems that managing rental properties usually presents.
7. Even the bad renter situation made me a lot of money.
8. If a rental goes bad, I have several options: rent, sell, or trade.
9. I designed the plan to benefit me even if someone rented for two years and backed out of the contract. In that situation, I can re-rent the property and get 14 years rent instead of 12.
10. Even if the property is not in the best condition, this plan gives the renters high motivation to make the repairs.
11. Houses remained at low prices over a long period.
12. I am more flexible than banks, which makes for good relationships with renters.
13. There is no down payment, which attracts renters.

14. There is no security deposit, which attracts renters.
15. My customers are grateful. This rent-to-barter deal is probably their only chance to own a home.
16. It makes dealing with renters easy.
17. Renters are not burdened with taxes and insurances until the home is theirs.

    I am not the only one who likes the plan, renters like it and bankers do too. I was in the bank seeking an equity line on one of my houses and had my financial statement to show the bank. I was dealing with a new employee who was having trouble with the computer, so he called over the bank manager to help. When they got the computer fixed he (the manager) wanted to see my financial statement. He looked it over and said, "I see you make a lot of money. How many years did it take you to do this." I told him three years and he said, "You did that in three years. I want to know how. My father has $1,000,000 invested and he doesn't make anywhere near what you are making." So, I took some time and explained my plan to him.

    I purchased a property for my daughter and spent seven months remodeling it so she would have almost no maintenance problems. She decided the property did not fit her needs. She thought two acres was too small, so I put it on one of my 12-year rental plans and we found a second ranch. This property was almost 12 acres and included a two-acre lake stocked with large fish. It also had a 2,000 square foot upscale house, a 55'x72' modern barn and a 24'x60' barn. It also had a storm cellar, a 24x48 garage shop, a 100 yard paved driveway, a large brick entry with a steel gate and 1000' of welded 4 bar 1.25" almost new steel fencing along the front. It sat on a small hill and looked majestic. In Orange County, California, it would sell for well over a million dollars, but not in the country in Humansville, Missouri. My daughter also turned down this property so I tried to sell it. I could not get a buyer for $165,000 even though it was a well-kept property. Family incomes there are very low and there are very few who can afford that much property or the down payment to get a loan.

I decided to put it on Craig's List on one of my 12-year deals at a rent value in line with the sale value of $165,000. In the ad, I included the phone numbers for both my cell phone and our home phone in California. I laid the phones on a table in the backyard near where I was working. Both phones rang at the same time. I answered one and the party said they wanted to take my deal. I asked them to wait a moment so that I could take the call on my other phone. That party said they wanted to take my deal, so I held the phones together and talked to both. In ten minutes, the price on which the rent would be based went from $165,000 to $185,000.

My conclusions about this investment plan are: it has high demand, it is easy to run, it requires none of the usual costs of renting, and as soon as I finish paying the mortgages, this plan will give me all the money I need to spend for the balance of my life. Even now, I can spend more as I choose. This investment has made me 20% during the recession when others were making 2 or 3% or less. I plan to share my good fortune with my family, the church, and especially the grandkids who are just starting their families. It will help them when they need it most.

If you would like to know more or buy a book, call me at (951) 925-6108 or on my cell: (951) 663-0139.

www.ingramcontent.com/pod-product-compliance
Lightning Source LLC
Chambersburg PA
CBHW030049230526
45471CB00003B/1004